Real Size S

Rocks and Soil

Rebecca Rissman

Raintree

Raintree is an imprint of Capstone Global Library
Limited, a company incorporated in England and Wales
having its registered office at 7 Pilgrim Street, London,
EC4V 6LB – Registered company number: 6695582

www.raintreepublishers.co.uk
myorders@raintreepublishers.co.uk

Edited by Rebecca Rissman, Daniel Nunn,
    and John-Paul Wilkins
Designed by Joanna Malivoire and Tim Bond
Picture research by Ruth Blaire
Production by Sophia Argyris
Originated by Capstone Global Library Ltd
Printed and bound in China by South China
    Printing Company

ISBN 978 1 406 26352 7 (hardback)
17 16 15 14 13
10 9 8 7 6 5 4 3 2 1

ISBN 978 1 406 26359 6 (paperback)
18 17 16 15 14
10 9 8 7 6 5 4 3 2 1

British Library Cataloguing in Publication Data
Rissman, Rebecca.
Rocks and soil. – (Real size science)
552-dc23
A full catalogue record for this book is available from
the British Library.

Acknowledgements
We would like to thank the following for permission to
reproduce photographs: Getty Images pp. 11 main
(Jaime Kowal), 19 (S. Meltzer), 21 (Mario Tama), 22
(Tim Graham); Shutterstock pp. 4 (© gkuna), 5
(© Losevsky Photo and Video), 6 (© B Calkins), 7
(© Alistair Scott), 8 (© lenetstan), 9 (© Larisa Lofitskaya),
10 (© Roberto Caucino), 11 (© Pablo Hidalgo), 12
(© Robert Adrian Hillman), 13 (© LesPalenik), 14
(© Alina Cardiae Photography), 15 (© Andriano),
16 (© marionhassold), 17 (© Maryna Pleshkun), 18
(© Phaitoon Sutunyawatchai), 20 fossils (© Eduardo
Rivero) 20 sand background (© keren-seg).

Cover photograph of a fold of fossil shells reproduced
with permission of Shutterstock (© AleZanIT).

We would like to thank Dee Reid and Nancy Harris for
their invaluable help in the preparation of this book.

Every effort has been made to contact copyright holders
of material reproduced in this book. Any omissions will
be rectified in subsequent printings if notice is given to
the publisher.

Contents

Rocks and soil
Rocks and soil are found in nature.

There are many different types of rocks and soil.

Real size

Soil

Soil is made of pieces of dead plants, animals, and small rocks.

Plants need soil to grow.

Soil can be dry.

Real size

Soil can be wet.

Rocks

There are different types of rocks.

Real Size

magma

Igneous rock is made from cooled magma.

Sedimentary rock is made from tiny pieces of soil and rocks that have been squeezed together.

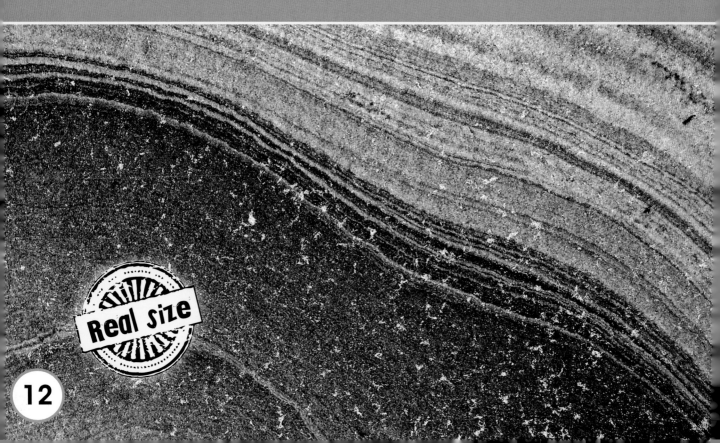

Real size

Metamorphic rock is rock that has changed from another type of rock.

Some rocks are beautiful.
They can be worn as gemstones.

Sand

Sand is made of small pieces of shells and rock.

Some sand is made from very small pieces.

Real size

Some sand is made from bigger pieces of stones and shells.

Real Size

Fossils

Fossils are parts of animals or plants. They are found in rock.

Fossils are very old.

Some fossils are small.
This animal is called a trilobite.

Real size

Some fossils are large.
This tooth is part of a
Tyrannosaurus rex fossil.

Real size surprise!

This diamond is a valuable rock. It is in the Queen Mother's crown.

Real Size

diamond

Picture glossary

 **fossil** remains or trace of a living thing from the past in rock or soil

 **gemstone** valuable stone used for jewellery

 **magma** hot liquid rock beneath Earth's surface. Magma that comes out of volcanoes is called lava.

Index

Notes for parents and teachers

Before reading

- Engage children in a discussion about size. Ask children to think of different ways we describe size, such as tall, short, wide, or thin.
- Tell children that we can use tools, such as rulers to measure size. We can also use body parts, such as hand lengths and foot lengths to measure size.

After reading

- Ask children to turn to pages 16–17. Which photo shows sand with larger pieces? Do children need to use a ruler to measure this, or can they tell just by looking?
- Ask children to turn to page 21. Using a ruler, ask children to measure the length of the Tyrannosaurus rex tooth. Then ask them to measure the tooth using their hand length (e.g., one hand length long, or one and a half hand lengths long).